HERBAL EXPLORERS:

A Children's Guide to Herbalism

Emily Kate Adams

Herbal Press

ISBN-13: 9798332588778
ISBN-10: 1477123456

Cover design by: Herbal Press
Library of Congress Control Number: 2018675309
Printed in the United States of America

CONTENTS

LEGAL DISCLAIMER:

The information provided in this book, "Herbal Explorers: A Children's Guide to Herbalism," is intended for educational purposes only. It is not meant to replace the advice of a qualified healthcare professional.

The authors and publishers of this book have made every effort to ensure that the information provided is accurate and up to date at the time of publication. However, they make no representations or warranties of any kind, express or implied, about the completeness, accuracy, reliability, suitability, or availability with respect to the information, products, services, or related graphics contained in this book for any purpose.

Any reliance you place on such information is strictly at your own risk. The authors and publishers will not be liable for any loss or damage, including without limitation, indirect or consequential loss or damage, or any loss or damage whatsoever arising from loss of data or profits arising out of, or in connection with, the use of this book.

WELCOME TO THE WORLD OF HERBALISM

Welcome, dear young friends, to a world filled with excitement and mystery—the enchanting realm of herbalism! Have you ever wondered what herbalism is? Well, let me tell you! Herbalism is like a special kind of magic. It's all about using plants—like leaves, flowers, and roots—to help us feel better and stay healthy.

Imagine this: long, long ago, even before there were hospitals and doctors like we have today, people used plants as their medicine. For thousands of years, plants have been our helpers, giving us strength and healing. Think of herbalism as a journey into a magical garden where every plant is a tiny superhero, ready to come to our rescue when we're sick or feeling blue.

In this special garden, every leaf, petal, and stem has a secret power waiting to be discovered. Picture yourself surrounded by colorful flowers, each one whispering its own unique secret. There's calming lavender, which can help you feel relaxed and peaceful, and refreshing peppermint, which can make your tummy feel better when it's upset. Each herb is like a little treasure just waiting for us to find it and learn its special gift.

But wait, there's more! Herbalism isn't just about using plants for medicine. It's also about exploring nature and learning about the amazing things plants can do. As we wander through the garden, we'll discover how plants grow, what they need to stay healthy, and how they can help us in so many different ways. We'll learn about the sun, water, and soil—everything plants need to be happy and strong.

Now, let's talk about the science behind herbalism. Plants are like tiny factories, making special substances called "compounds" that can help us. These compounds can have different effects on our bodies. For example, when you smell a flower, you're actually smelling some of these compounds. Some compounds can make us feel better, like the ones in chamomile that help us relax. Scientists study these compounds to understand how they work. This helps us know which plants are best for different things, like soothing a sore throat or helping a cut heal faster.

Imagine being able to make your own herbal remedies, like a potion-making wizard! You could create a soothing tea from chamomile to help you sleep better or a minty balm to cool a bug bite. We'll learn how to pick the right plants, dry them, and use them to make our own magical concoctions. And we'll also learn about how these plant compounds work in our bodies to help us feel better.

As we explore the world of herbalism, we'll learn how plants grow. Did you know that plants need sunlight, water, and nutrients from the soil to grow strong and healthy? We'll find out how roots take in water and nutrients, how leaves make food for the plant through a process called photosynthesis, and how flowers can turn into fruits and seeds.

We'll also discover the different parts of plants and how each part can be used in herbalism. Leaves, flowers, roots, and seeds can all have different uses. For example, the roots of a plant called echinacea can help boost our immune system, while the flowers of the calendula plant can be used to make a healing cream for our skin.

We'll also meet some of the people who use herbalism in their everyday lives. These people are called herbalists. Herbalists are like plant detectives. They know all about the different plants and how to use them to help people feel better. Some herbalists work in gardens, growing and harvesting plants. Others might work in shops, helping people find the right herbs for their needs. Some even travel the world, discovering new plants and learning about different ways to use them.

So, my dear friends, are you ready to embark on a magical adventure? Together, we'll explore the secrets of herbalism, learn about the amazing powers of plants, and maybe even make some herbal remedies of our own. We'll become like plant detectives, discovering the wonders of nature and learning how to use plants to help us stay healthy and happy.

Are you excited? Then let's dive in and begin our journey through the wonderful world of herbalism!

MEET SOME COMMON HERBS

L et's embark on an adventure through the garden of herbs!

1. Lavender

Imagine a field full of little purple flowers, swaying gently in the breeze like a fairy dance. Lavender is one of these lovely flowers, and it brings calm and peace wherever it goes!

What Makes Lavender Special?
Soothing Scent:
Lavender has a sweet scent that's like taking a deep breath of fresh air on a sunny day. It's so soothing and comforting!
When you smell lavender, it's like wrapping yourself

in a cozy blanket of calmness. It helps you feel relaxed and peaceful, like sitting by a quiet lake on a summer afternoon.

Uses of Lavender:
Beauty Products: You can find lavender in things like soap and lotion. These products not only make your skin feel soft but also smell nice and calming, just like a gentle hug for your body.
Bedtime Buddy: Some people put dried lavender flowers in a little pouch and tuck it into their pillows at night. The soothing scent helps them relax and sleep better, like having a tiny bedtime buddy whispering sweet dreams in your ear.

Growing Lavender:
Lavender plants grow best in sunny spots with well-drained soil. They love to soak up the sunshine and sway in the breeze.
You can even grow your own lavender plant in a garden or pot at home! It's like having your own little piece of calmness right outside your window.

Lavender in Nature
Lavender isn't just pretty; it's also important for bees and butterflies. They love to visit lavender flowers to collect nectar and pollen, helping plants grow new seeds.
The purple flowers attract these helpful insects, making lavender a favorite spot in the garden for both people and wildlife.

Learning from Lavender
Relaxation: Lavender teaches us to slow down and take a deep breath, just like it does in the garden. It reminds us to relax and enjoy moments of peace.
Nature's Gift: By enjoying lavender's calming scent and beauty, we learn to appreciate nature's gifts and how they can help us feel happy and well.

Fun Fact!
Did you know? Lavender is not just a pretty flower —it's also a herb! People have been using lavender for centuries to make teas, oils, and even delicious treats like lavender cookies and lemonade.

Next time you see a lavender plant or smell its sweet scent, take a moment to breathe it in. Let its calming magic wash over you, like a gentle hug from nature reminding us to relax and enjoy the beauty around us.

2. Peppermint

Imagine a plant with bright green leaves and a fresh, minty scent that tickles your nose—this is peppermint! Peppermint is like nature's own cool breeze, bringing freshness and joy wherever it grows.

What Makes Peppermint Special?
Cooling Minty Scent:
Peppermint has a refreshing scent that's like a burst of coolness in the air. When you smell peppermint, it wakes up your senses and makes you feel alert and alive, like a splash of cold water on a hot day.

Uses of Peppermint:
Refreshing Tea: People love to make peppermint tea by steeping the leaves in hot water. It's not only tasty but also soothing for your tummy, like a warm hug from the inside.
Candy and Treats: Peppermint is also used to make yummy candies, like candy canes during the holidays! These treats are sweet and refreshing, making them a favorite for celebrations.

Growing Peppermint:
Peppermint plants grow best in sunny to partially shaded spots with moist soil. They spread quickly and send up tall stems with leaves that smell amazing when you touch them.

You can grow peppermint in a garden or a pot at home. It's easy to care for and adds a burst of fresh scent to your outdoor space or kitchen window.

Peppermint in Nature
Peppermint isn't just tasty; it's also helpful for bees and butterflies. They visit peppermint flowers to collect nectar and pollen, helping plants grow new seeds.

The flowers attract these helpful insects, making peppermint a buzzing hub of activity in gardens, which helps plants and wildlife thrive.

Learning from Peppermint
Alertness: Peppermint teaches us to feel awake and refreshed, just like its cool scent. It reminds us to be alert and ready for new adventures.

Nature's Sweetness: By enjoying peppermint's fresh scent and taste, we learn to appreciate nature's flavors and how they can make us feel happy and healthy.

Fun Fact!
Did you know? Peppermint isn't just for tea and candy—it's also used in things like toothpaste and gum to make your mouth feel clean and fresh.

Next time you smell peppermint or sip peppermint tea, think about its cool and refreshing magic. Let its invigorating scent fill you with energy and joy, like a burst of freshness from nature.

3. Chamomile

Imagine a sunny garden filled with small, daisy-like flowers that smell sweet and soothing—that's chamomile! Chamomile is like a gentle hug from nature, known for its calming and comforting qualities.

What Makes Chamomile Special?
Soothing Scent and Taste:
Chamomile has a gentle, flowery scent that's relaxing when you smell it. It's also used to make a delicious tea that tastes mild and slightly sweet, like a warm hug in a cup.

Uses of Chamomile:
Relaxing Tea: People love to brew chamomile tea by steeping the dried flowers in hot water. It's not just tasty but also helps you feel calm and cozy, perfect

before bedtime.

Skincare: Chamomile is used in lotions and creams because it's gentle and helps soothe skin. It's like giving your skin a gentle kiss from nature to keep it soft and happy.

Growing Chamomile:

Chamomile plants grow best in sunny spots with well-drained soil. They have pretty, daisy-like flowers that butterflies and bees love to visit.

You can grow chamomile in a garden or a pot at home. It's easy to care for and adds a touch of peacefulness to your outdoor space or windowsill.

Chamomile in Nature

Chamomile flowers are like a beacon for helpful insects, such as bees and butterflies. They visit the flowers to collect pollen and nectar, helping plants grow new seeds and keeping gardens buzzing with life.

Learning from Chamomile

Calming Influence: Chamomile teaches us to relax and unwind, like its gentle scent and soothing tea. It reminds us to take a deep breath and find peace in nature's embrace.

Nature's Gifts: By enjoying chamomile tea or using chamomile in skincare, we learn to appreciate nature's gifts and how they can make us feel calm and cared for.

Fun Fact!
Did you know? Chamomile has been used for centuries as a natural remedy to help people feel relaxed and happy. It's like a little flower friend that brings comfort wherever it grows.

Next time you see chamomile flowers or sip chamomile tea, think about their gentle and calming magic. Let their soothing presence wrap you in warmth and relaxation, like a gentle breeze from a sunny garden.

4. Rosemary
Imagine a sunny garden where fragrant green leaves tickle your nose—this is rosemary! Rosemary is like a green-fingered wizard, known for its wonderful smell and magical properties.

What Makes Rosemary Special?

Aromatic Herb:
Rosemary has needle-like leaves that smell like a mix of pine and lemon. It's a fragrant herb that adds a burst of freshness to the air.

Uses of Rosemary:
Flavorful Cooking: People love to sprinkle rosemary on roasted potatoes or chicken to make them taste delicious and savory, like a secret ingredient from nature's pantry.
Herbal Remedies: Rosemary is used in natural remedies for its soothing properties. It can be made into a tea that helps with digestion or used in essential oils to promote relaxation.

Growing Rosemary:
Rosemary plants thrive in sunny spots with well-drained soil. They grow as small shrubs with woody stems and delicate blue flowers that bees adore.
You can grow rosemary in a garden or a pot on your windowsill. It's easy to care for and adds a touch of magic to your cooking and home.

Rosemary in Nature
Rosemary bushes are like bustling cities for helpful insects, such as bees and butterflies. They visit the flowers to collect nectar, making gardens lively and buzzing with activity.

Learning from Rosemary
Flavorful Fun: Rosemary teaches us that herbs can

make food taste amazing and bring joy to cooking. It's like adding a sprinkle of magic to every meal.

Natural Wellness: By using rosemary in teas or oils, we learn about its healing properties and how nature provides us with remedies to stay healthy and happy.

Fun Fact!

Did you know? Ancient Greeks and Romans believed rosemary had powers to improve memory. They wore rosemary garlands on their heads during exams to help them remember facts—like having a brain-boosting herb on their side!

Next time you smell rosemary or cook with it, think about its fragrant and magical qualities. Let its fresh aroma and tasty flavor inspire you to explore the wonders of herbs in your everyday life.

5. Thyme

Imagine a garden filled with tiny green leaves that smell like a mix of mint and lemon—that's thyme! Thyme is like a little garden fairy, spreading its delicious aroma wherever it grows.

What Makes Thyme Special?

Aromatic Herb:
Thyme has small, green leaves that release a delightful scent when you rub them between your fingers. It smells fresh and herbal, like a walk through a sunny garden.

Uses of Thyme:
Flavorful Cooking: People love to sprinkle thyme on roasted vegetables or soups to make them taste savory and delicious, adding a burst of flavor like magic dust from nature's kitchen.
Herbal Remedies: Thyme is used in teas and as an essential oil for its calming properties. It can help you relax and feel cozy, like a warm hug from nature.

Growing Thyme:
Thyme plants are small shrubs that love sunny spots with well-drained soil. They grow close to the ground, with tiny flowers that attract bees and butterflies.
You can grow thyme in a garden or a pot on your windowsill. It's easy to care for and brings a touch of herbal charm to your cooking and home.

Thyme in Nature
Thyme bushes are like bustling cities for helpful insects, such as bees and butterflies. They visit the flowers to collect nectar, making gardens lively and buzzing with activity.

Learning from Thyme
Flavorful Fun: Thyme teaches us that herbs can make food taste amazing and bring joy to cooking. It's like adding a sprinkle of magic to every meal.
Natural Wellness: By using thyme in teas or oils, we learn about its calming properties and how nature provides us with remedies to feel relaxed and happy.

Fun Fact!
Did you know? Ancient Egyptians used thyme in their embalming process to preserve mummies! It was believed to have magical powers to protect and purify.

Next time you smell thyme or cook with it, think about its fresh and magical qualities. Let its aromatic scent and tasty flavor inspire you to explore the wonders of herbs in your everyday life.

6. Lemon Balm

Imagine a plant with bright green leaves that smell like a fresh lemonade on a hot summer day—that's lemon balm! Lemon balm is like a burst of sunshine in your garden, bringing a refreshing citrus scent wherever it grows.

What Makes Lemon Balm Special?
Citrusy Aroma:
Lemon balm has soft, fuzzy leaves that release a lemony scent when you rub them. It smells sweet and tangy, like squeezing a lemon slice.

Uses of Lemon Balm:
Refreshing Tea: People love to make tea with lemon balm leaves. It tastes soothing and can help you feel calm and happy, like sipping sunshine in a cup.
Natural Bug Repellent: Lemon balm is also used to keep bugs away. Its lemony scent can ward

off mosquitoes and other pesky insects, making outdoor adventures more enjoyable.

Growing Lemon Balm:
Lemon balm plants are easy to grow in gardens or pots. They like sunny spots with well-drained soil and can grow tall with small clusters of white flowers that bees love.
You can plant lemon balm in your garden to attract friendly pollinators like bees, helping plants grow and making your garden buzz with life.

Lemon Balm in Nature
Lemon balm bushes are like little lemon-scented oases for bees and butterflies. They visit the flowers to collect nectar, making gardens lively with their buzzing and fluttering.

Learning from Lemon Balm
Sunny Scent: Lemon balm teaches us that herbs can smell and taste like our favorite fruits, adding fun flavors to teas and natural bug repellents.
Garden Helpers: By growing lemon balm, we learn about helping plants and pollinators thrive together in our gardens, creating a happy and buzzing habitat.

Fun Fact!
Did you know? Lemon balm has been used since ancient times by people like the Romans and Greeks to soothe their minds and bodies. They believed

it had magical powers to lift spirits and bring happiness.

Next time you see lemon balm or make tea with it, think about its sunny and refreshing qualities. Let its citrusy aroma and calming flavor inspire you to explore the wonders of herbs in your everyday life.

7. Echinacea

Imagine a flower that looks like a colorful pinwheel spinning in the wind—that's echinacea! Echinacea is like a superhero plant in our gardens, helping us stay strong and healthy.

What Makes Echinacea Special?
Beautiful Flower:

Echinacea has bright purple or pink petals that look like a daisy with a spiky center. It grows tall and strong, waving in the breeze like a friendly garden sentinel.

Health Benefits:
Immune Booster: Echinacea is famous for helping our bodies fight off bad germs. When we feel a little under the weather, echinacea can give our immune systems a boost, like a superhero saving the day!
Soothing Tea: People also make tea with echinacea flowers and roots. It tastes a bit earthy and can help us feel better when we have a scratchy throat or a sniffly nose.

Growing Echinacea:
Echinacea loves sunny spots in gardens or big pots. It likes soil that drains well and doesn't like to sit in water too long. With a little water and sunshine, echinacea can grow big and healthy, attracting butterflies and bees with its bright colors.

Echinacea in Nature
Echinacea flowers are like beacons for butterflies and bees. They visit the flowers to collect sweet nectar and carry pollen from flower to flower, helping plants make seeds.

Learning from Echinacea
Superhero Strength: Echinacea teaches us that plants can be like superheroes, helping us stay healthy and strong.
Garden Guardians: By growing echinacea, we learn about caring for plants and creating habitats for

helpful insects like butterflies and bees.

Fun Fact!
Did you know? Native American tribes have used echinacea for centuries to support their health. They believed it had special powers to boost their immune systems and keep them strong.

Next time you see echinacea in a garden or make tea with it, think about its superhero qualities. Let its colorful petals and earthy flavor remind you of the plant superheroes that help us feel good and keep our gardens buzzing with life.

8. Dandelion
Imagine a flower that looks like a burst of sunshine in your backyard—that's a dandelion! Let's uncover the magic and wonders of this humble plant.

What Makes Dandelions Special?
Bright and Cheerful:
Dandelions have bright yellow flowers that pop up in grassy fields, parks, and even in cracks in sidewalks. They're like little bursts of sunshine on the ground!

Every Part is Useful:
Flowers: Bees and butterflies love to visit dandelion flowers for nectar. They help pollinate other plants, which means more flowers and fruits grow in our gardens.
Leaves: Dandelion leaves are like nutritious greens! Some people add them to salads for a crunchy, slightly bitter taste. They're packed with vitamins and minerals that are good for our bodies.
Roots: Under the ground, dandelion roots are long and strong. People sometimes dry and grind them into a powder. It can be used to make tea that's soothing and helps our tummies feel better.

Fun in the Wind:
Have you ever blown on a dandelion puff? Each white puffball is full of tiny seeds. When you blow on it, the seeds float away like tiny parachutes, spreading dandelion plants to new places.

Dandelions in Nature
Dandelions are like little ecosystems in themselves. They provide food for insects, nutrients for the soil when their leaves decompose, and even medicine for

people who use them for tea.

Learning from Dandelions
Nature's Helpers: Dandelions teach us that even common plants have special powers to help nature and people.
Exploring Outdoors: Look for dandelions in your neighborhood or local park. See how many different stages of growth you can find—from bright yellow flowers to fluffy white seeds.

Fun Fact!
Did you know? Dandelions are one of the first flowers bees visit in the spring because they provide important early-season nectar and pollen.

Next time you see a dandelion, think about its sunny yellow flowers, nutritious leaves, and fluffy seeds. Dandelions aren't just weeds; they're important parts of our natural world that bring joy, food, and even health benefits.

9. Calendula

Imagine a flower that shines like the sun and helps people feel better—that's calendula! Let's uncover the magic and wonders of this special plant.

What Makes Calendula Special?
Sunshine in Petals:
Calendula flowers look like little bursts of sunshine in gardens and fields. They come in bright shades of yellow and orange, making them stand out wherever they bloom.

Healing Powers:
Skin Soothing: Calendula petals are used to make creams and ointments that help soothe skin. When people have cuts, scrapes, or dry skin, calendula can help them feel better faster.
Gentle Medicine: Some people drink calendula tea to help with tummy troubles or to calm down when

feeling a bit anxious. It's like having a warm hug from nature inside.

Garden Friend:
Calendula plants aren't just pretty; they're also good for other plants. They attract helpful insects like bees and butterflies that pollinate gardens and help fruits and vegetables grow.

Calendula in Nature
Calendula plants are like little helpers in gardens. They don't just look pretty; they also work hard to make sure gardens stay healthy and happy.

Learning from Calendula
Nature's Doctor: Calendula teaches us that plants can be like medicine, helping us feel better and taking care of our bodies.
Exploring Gardens: Look for calendula flowers in gardens or parks. Notice their bright colors and how they attract insects that help flowers bloom.

Fun Fact!
Did you know? Calendula flowers are edible! You can sprinkle the petals on salads or use them to decorate cakes for a sunny touch.

Next time you see a calendula flower, think about its bright colors, healing powers, and how it helps other plants and insects. Calendula isn't just a flower; it's a helpful friend in gardens and a gentle healer for people.

10. Sage

Let's dive into the world of sage—a herb that's not just for cooking but also for feeling good inside and out!

Discovering Sage
Aromatic Wonder:
Sage is like a fragrant superstar in the herb world. Its leaves are soft and fuzzy, and when you touch them, they release a fresh, earthy smell that's calming and refreshing.
Cooking Magic:
People love to cook with sage because it adds a special flavor to foods. Imagine sprinkling sage into soups or on roasted potatoes—it makes everything taste warm and delicious!

Healing Powers:
Soothing Tea: Sage tea isn't just tasty; it's good for your throat when it's feeling scratchy. It's like a cozy blanket for your insides!
Natural Medicine: Sage has been used for centuries to help with things like digestion and to make people feel better when they're not quite themselves.

Sage in Nature
Sage plants grow in gardens and wild spaces where they soak up the sun and share their soothing scent with everyone around them.

Learning from Sage
Herbal Helper: Sage teaches us that herbs can do more than just taste good—they can also help us feel better inside.
Cooking Adventures: Ask your parents to try cooking with sage at home. You can help sprinkle it into dishes and taste how it changes the flavors.

Fun Fact!
Did you know? Native American cultures used sage in ceremonies to cleanse spaces and people's spirits, believing it brought wisdom and clarity.

Next time you see sage in a garden or smell it in your kitchen, think about its calming scent and how it makes food taste so yummy. Sage isn't just a herb; it's a helper in the kitchen and a friend to anyone who needs a little soothing.

11. Nettle

Let's delve into the fascinating world of nettle—a resilient herb that offers both nutritional benefits and healing properties!

Discovering Nettle
Nutrient Powerhouse:
Nettle leaves are like nature's multivitamin! They're packed with essential nutrients such as iron, vitamin C, vitamin K, and several minerals like calcium and magnesium. These nutrients help our bodies grow strong, support our immune system, and keep our bones healthy.

Versatile Uses:
Despite its stinging reputation, nettle is a versatile herb used in culinary and medicinal practices. It can be cooked and eaten like spinach or brewed into a nourishing tea. The dried leaves are also used in

herbal infusions and supplements for their health benefits.

Historical and Cultural Significance:
Throughout history, nettle has been valued for its medicinal properties. Ancient civilizations used nettle to treat various ailments, from joint pain to allergies. It was also used as a nutritious food source and even to make fabric!

Nettle in Nature
Nettle plants thrive in temperate regions around the world, often growing in moist, nutrient-rich soil. They can be found in gardens, forests, and along riverbanks, providing habitat and food for insects and small animals.

Learning from Nettle
Health Benefits: Nettle teaches us about the importance of incorporating nutrient-rich herbs into our diets for overall health and well-being.
Gardening Fun: Consider growing nettle in a garden or observing it in its natural habitat. It's a hands-on way to learn about plant life cycles and herbal medicine.

Fun Fact!
Did you know? Nettle has been used for centuries as a natural dye for fabrics. It produces a vibrant green color when processed correctly, showcasing its versatility beyond medicinal and culinary uses.

Nettle is more than just a herb—it's a symbol of resilience and nutritional richness in the world of herbalism. Whether brewed into a soothing tea or added to a savory dish, nettle offers a taste of nature's bounty and a boost of essential nutrients.

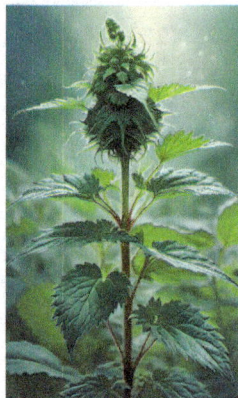

12. Ginger

Let's journey into the world of ginger—a versatile root celebrated for its unique flavor and powerful medicinal properties.

Discovering Ginger
Flavorful Spice:
Ginger is known for its zesty and slightly spicy flavor. It adds a kick to dishes and beverages, making it a favorite in cuisines around the world. From stir-fries to gingerbread cookies, its versatility in cooking is unmatched!

Medicinal Marvel:
Beyond its culinary use, ginger has been used for centuries in traditional medicine for its healing properties. It's known to aid digestion, reduce nausea, and alleviate inflammation and pain. Ginger tea is a popular remedy for soothing upset stomachs and easing cold symptoms.

Rich History:
Ginger has a rich history dating back thousands of years. It originated in Southeast Asia and has been traded and valued across ancient civilizations for its medicinal and culinary benefits. Today, it's cultivated in many tropical regions worldwide.

Ginger in Nature
Ginger plants (Zingiber officinale) grow in tropical climates, thriving in warm and humid conditions. The plant's rhizome (underground stem) is harvested for culinary and medicinal purposes, highlighting its importance in both traditional and modern herbalism.

Learning from Ginger
Health Benefits: Ginger teaches us about natural remedies for digestive health, inflammation, and immune support.

Fun Fact!
Did you know? Ginger is a flowering plant related to turmeric, cardamom, and galangal—all part of the

Zingiberaceae family. Its unique aroma and flavor make it a staple in spice blends and herbal remedies.

Ginger is more than just a spice—it's a powerhouse of flavor and health benefits. Whether enjoyed in tea, added to savory dishes, or used in desserts, ginger offers a burst of zest and wellness in every bite.

13. Oregano
Let's delve into the world of oregano—a beloved herb known for its robust flavor and therapeutic qualities.

Discovering Oregano
Flavorful Herb:
Oregano is celebrated for its strong, aromatic flavor reminiscent of the Mediterranean. It adds depth to dishes like pizza, pasta sauces, and salads, earning

its place as a staple in Italian and Greek cuisines.

Medicinal Marvel:
Beyond its culinary use, oregano has been valued for its medicinal properties for centuries. It contains antioxidants and compounds that may have antibacterial and anti-inflammatory effects. Oregano oil, extracted from the leaves, is used in natural remedies for respiratory issues and digestive discomfort.

Cultural Heritage:
Oregano has deep roots in Mediterranean cultures, where it grows abundantly in sunny climates. It's traditionally harvested and dried for culinary and medicinal purposes, reflecting its importance in ancient herbal traditions.

Oregano in Nature
Oregano (Origanum vulgare) is a perennial herb that thrives in well-drained soil and full sunlight. Its small, aromatic leaves are rich in essential oils, which contribute to its distinctive flavor and therapeutic benefits.

Fun Fact!
Did you know? Oregano is often associated with joy and happiness in Mediterranean folklore. It's used in festivals and celebrations to bring good fortune and prosperity.

Oregano is more than just an herb—it's a symbol of culinary richness and wellness. Whether used fresh or dried, oregano adds a burst of flavor and health benefits to dishes, embodying the essence of Mediterranean cuisine.

GROWING YOUR OWN HERBAL GARDEN

Become a Green-Fingered Herbalist and Grow Your Own Herbal Paradise! Imagine stepping into a world where you can grow your own magical herbs, right at home! From the fragrant basil to the delicious mint, you can create a beautiful herb garden that not only looks amazing but also provides fresh herbs for your recipes and natural remedies. Are you ready to become a green-fingered gardener? Let's get started on this exciting adventure with your parents!

Steps to Growing Your Own Herbal Garden

1. Choose a Sunny Spot

Before starting your herb garden adventure, gather with your parents to find the perfect spot. Take a walk around your home—maybe there's a sunny corner in your backyard, a bright balcony, or a sunny windowsill indoors. Your parents can teach you about sunlight and why it's important for plants. Together, observe how the sunlight moves throughout the day, and choose a spot where your herbs can soak up at least 6 hours of sunshine. This sunny spot will be the perfect home for your herb garden!

Why Sunlight is Important for Plants

Plants need sunlight to grow and stay healthy. The process by which they use sunlight to make their own food is called photosynthesis. Let's learn a bit more about this fascinating process:

Photosynthesis:
What is it? Photosynthesis is like a magical kitchen inside the plant's leaves. Plants use sunlight to turn carbon dioxide (a gas from the air) and water into food (sugar) and oxygen.
How does it work? Inside the leaves are tiny parts called chloroplasts, which contain a green pigment called chlorophyll. Chlorophyll captures the sunlight and uses its energy to mix carbon dioxide and water, creating sugar for the plant to eat and oxygen for us to breathe.

Parts of the Plant Involved in Photosynthesis:

Leaves: The main part where photosynthesis happens. Leaves have special cells that contain chlorophyll.
Roots: They take up water and minerals from the soil, which are necessary for photosynthesis.
Stems: They support the plant and transport water and nutrients from the roots to the leaves.

Why Plants Need Sunlight:

Food Production: Just like we need food to grow and have energy, plants need to make their own food. Without sunlight, they can't produce the energy they need.
Growth: Sunlight helps plants grow strong and healthy. Without enough sunlight, plants can become weak and may not grow properly.
Flowering and Fruiting: Sunlight helps plants produce flowers and fruits. These are important for making new plants and providing us with fruits and vegetables.

Observing the Sunlight:

With your parents, spend a day observing how the sunlight moves around your home. Here's what to do:

Morning Observation:

Go outside or look out the window early in the morning.
Notice which areas get the first light of the day. These spots are usually on the east side.

Midday Observation:
Check again around noon.
See where the sunlight is strongest. This is usually the south-facing areas because the sun is high in the sky.

Afternoon Observation:
Look again in the late afternoon.
Notice which areas are still sunny and which ones are in shade. The west side usually gets the afternoon sun.

Recording Your Observations:
Draw a simple map of your home and mark the sunny spots at different times of the day.
Use symbols like a sun ☀ for sunny spots and a cloud ☁ for shaded areas.

Choosing the Perfect Spot:

After observing the sunlight, gather with your parents to choose the best spot for your herb garden. Here are some tips:

Sunny Corner in the Backyard: If you have a backyard, find a spot that gets at least 6 hours of sunlight. It could be near a fence or in a garden bed.

Bright Balcony: If you live in an apartment, a sunny balcony can be perfect. Make sure it gets enough sunlight throughout the day.

Sunny Windowsill Indoors: If you're growing herbs inside, choose a windowsill that faces south or west to get plenty of sunlight.

By choosing a sunny spot, you'll give your herbs the best chance to grow big and strong, just like superheroes powered by the sun!

2. Prepare the Soil

Now it's time to get your hands dirty! With your parents' help, select a big pot, a planter box, or a patch of soil in your garden. Your parents can guide you in picking the right kind of soil for your herbs. They'll show you how to fill your pot or planter box with soil, making sure it's nice and fluffy so your herbs' roots can stretch out and grow. Together, mix in some compost or organic matter to give your herbs the nutrients they need to thrive. Preparing the soil is like getting the bed ready for your plants so they can sleep well and grow strong.

Understanding Soil:

Soil is like the foundation for your plants. It's where they get their nutrients, water, and a place for their roots to grow. Let's learn more about soil and how to prepare it for your herb garden:

Types of Soil:

Clay Soil: This soil is heavy and sticky. It holds water well but can become compacted, making it hard for roots to grow.

Sandy Soil: This soil is light and gritty. It drains water quickly but doesn't hold nutrients well.

Loamy Soil: This soil is a mix of sand, silt, and clay. It holds water and nutrients well and is perfect for growing plants. This is the best type of soil for your herb garden.

What Makes Soil Healthy?:

Texture: Healthy soil should be crumbly and fluffy, so roots can easily grow through it.

Nutrients: Soil should have nutrients like nitrogen, phosphorus, and potassium, which plants need to grow.

Drainage: Soil should be able to hold enough water for the plants but also let excess water drain away to prevent the roots from rotting.

Preparing the Soil:

With your parents, follow these steps to prepare the soil for your herb garden:

Selecting a Container or Patch:

Big Pot: Choose a pot that has drainage holes at the bottom to let excess water escape.

Planter Box: A wooden or plastic box that can hold

soil and has drainage holes.
Garden Patch: A section of your backyard where you can plant directly into the ground.

Choosing the Right Soil:
Potting Mix: If you're using pots or planter boxes, use a high-quality potting mix. This mix is specially designed to provide good drainage and aeration.
Garden Soil: If you're planting in the ground, use loamy soil or improve your existing soil by adding compost or organic matter.

Filling the Container or Preparing the Patch:
Fill the Pot or Planter Box: With your parents' help, fill your pot or planter box with soil. Make sure it's fluffy and not compacted.
Prepare the Garden Patch: If you're planting in the ground, use a shovel to turn over the soil, breaking up any clumps and removing rocks and weeds.

Adding Compost or Organic Matter:

Why Add Compost?: Compost is like a superfood for your soil. It's made of decomposed organic materials like leaves, grass clippings, and vegetable scraps. Compost adds nutrients to the soil and improves its texture.

How to Add Compost: Mix in a few handfuls of compost or organic matter into your soil. If you're using a pot or planter box, mix the compost evenly throughout the soil.

If you're preparing a garden patch, spread the compost over the soil and mix it in with a shovel or garden fork.

<u>Fun Soil Activities</u>

Here are some fun activities to do with your parents while preparing your soil:

Soil Texture Test:
Take a handful of soil and squeeze it in your hand.
If it stays together and feels sticky, it's clay soil.
If it falls apart easily and feels gritty, it's sandy soil.
If it holds together but crumbles when you poke it, it's loamy soil.

Worm Hunt:
Look for earthworms in your soil. Earthworms are great for the garden because they help break down organic matter and improve soil structure.
If you find any worms, gently place them back into the soil to help your garden grow.

Soil Layer Jar:
Fill a clear jar with soil from your garden.
Add water to the jar, close the lid, and shake it well.
Let the jar sit for a day, and then observe the layers that form. You'll see sand, silt, and clay layers settle at the bottom.

By preparing the soil properly, you'll give your herbs the best start in life, ensuring they have all the nutrients and support they need to grow big and strong.

3. Select Your Herbs

Gather with your parents and make a list of herbs you'd like to grow. Share your favorite foods and flavors with them, and they can help you choose herbs that will make your taste buds dance! Talk about each herb's special qualities—like how basil smells like pizza or how mint tastes like candy. Your parents can take you to a garden center or nursery to pick out your herb plants. It's like going on a treasure hunt for delicious flavors!

Choosing Your Herbs:
Now that you know more about some common herbs, it's time to choose which ones you want to grow. Here's how to make your selection:

Make a List:
Sit down with your parents and make a list of herbs you'd like to grow.
Think about your favorite foods and what herbs would go well with them. Do you love pizza? Basil would be perfect! Enjoy lemonade? Mint is a great choice!

Learn About Each Herb:
Research each herb on your list to learn about its special qualities and how to take care of it.
Look up pictures of the herbs to see what they look like and where they might fit best in your garden.

Visit a Garden Center or Nursery:
Your parents can take you to a garden center or nursery where you can see and smell the herbs in person.
It's like going on a treasure hunt! Look for healthy plants with green leaves and no signs of pests or disease.

Ask for Help:
Don't be afraid to ask the staff at the garden center for advice. They can tell you more about each herb and how to take care of it.
They might even have some tips on which herbs grow well together.

Fun Activities to Choose Your Herbs:

Here are some fun activities to do with your parents while choosing your herbs:

Herb Tasting:
Buy a few fresh herbs from the store and have a tasting session at home.
Try each herb on its own and then in different foods to see which ones you like best.

Herb Research Project:
Create a small booklet with pictures and information about each herb you want to grow. Include details like what the herb looks like, how it tastes, and what dishes it's used in.

Herb Drawing:
Draw pictures of the herbs you want to grow and label them with their names and special qualities. Hang your drawings in your garden area to remind you of your goals.

Plan Your Garden:
Draw a map of where you will plant each herb in your garden. Think about how big each plant will get and how much space they need to grow.

By selecting your herbs thoughtfully and learning about their special qualities, you'll be ready to grow a beautiful and delicious herb garden. Your herbs will not only add flavor to your meals but also teach you about nature and the joys of gardening. Happy herb hunting!

4. Plant Your Herbs

With your parents' guidance, it's time to get planting! They'll teach you how to gently remove each herb plant from its pot and help you dig little holes in the soil. Together, place each herb in its hole and cover its roots with soil. Your parents will show you how to pat the soil down gently to keep your herbs snug and cozy. Planting your herbs is like tucking them into bed—they'll be cozy and ready to grow!

Step-by-Step Guide to Planting Herbs

Gather Your Supplies:
Herb Plants: The herbs you chose at the garden center.
Trowel: A small hand shovel for digging holes.
Watering Can: For watering your herbs after planting.
Gardening Gloves: To protect your hands while working with soil.
Mulch (optional): To help retain moisture and keep weeds away.

Prepare the Planting Area:
For Pots or Planter Boxes: Make sure they are filled with the fluffy, prepared soil you worked on earlier.
For Garden Patches: Ensure the soil is loose and free of weeds or debris.

Learn About Root Systems:
Roots: The roots are like the plant's feet, anchoring it into the soil and taking up water and nutrients.
Root Ball: This is the mass of roots and soil that you see when you take the plant out of its pot.

Remove the Plant from Its Pot:
Gently Squeeze the Pot: Loosen the soil by gently squeezing the sides of the pot.
Tip and Slide: Tip the pot on its side and slide the plant out, supporting it with your hand. If it's stuck, you might need to tap the bottom of the pot.

Inspect the Roots:
Check the Root Ball: If the roots are tightly wound around the soil, this is called being "root-bound." You can gently tease some of the roots apart with your fingers to help them spread out in the soil.
Healthy Roots: Healthy roots are usually white or light-colored. They should not be dry or rotting.

Dig the Holes:
Use Your Trowel: Dig a hole in the soil that is just as deep and slightly wider than the root ball of your herb plant.
Spacing: Make sure to leave enough space between each plant so they have room to grow. A good rule of thumb is to space them about 12 inches apart.

Plant the Herbs:
Place the Herb in the Hole: Gently place the herb plant into the hole. The top of the root ball should be level with the soil surface.
Fill in the Soil: Fill in the soil around the root ball, pressing it down gently with your hands to remove any air pockets and ensure the plant is secure.

Fun Activities While Planting:
Here are some fun activities to do with your parents while planting your herbs:

Planting Song:
Make up a planting song or chant to sing while you work. This makes the activity fun and helps you remember the steps.

Herb Labeling:
Create labels for each of your herbs using popsicle sticks or small stones. Write the name of each herb and maybe even draw a small picture of the plant.

Herb Diary:
Start a herb diary where you can draw pictures of your herbs, write about the planting process, and track their growth over time.

Garden Scavenger Hunt:
After planting, have a garden scavenger hunt to find other interesting plants, insects, or rocks in your garden. This helps you learn more about the ecosystem around your herb garden.

By planting your herbs with care and attention, you'll create a beautiful, thriving herb garden. Your herbs will grow strong and healthy, ready to provide you with fresh flavors for your meals and a wonderful experience of nurturing living plants.

5. Water Your Garden

Now it's time to give your herb garden a drink! Grab a watering can, and with your parents' help, water your herbs right after planting. They'll show you how to water gently so you don't wash away the soil or hurt your plants. Your herbs will slurp up the water like they're taking a big gulp of refreshing juice! Make sure to water them regularly, especially on hot days, to keep them happy and hydrated.

Understanding the Importance of Water:
Water is essential for all living things, including plants. Here's why water is so important for your herb garden:

Hydration:
Just like you need water to stay hydrated, plants need water to help them grow and stay healthy. Water helps transport nutrients from the soil to the plant, supports photosynthesis (the process by which plants make their food), and keeps the plant cells strong and firm.

Nutrient Transport:
Water dissolves nutrients in the soil, making it easier for the roots to absorb them. Think of water as a delivery system that brings food to the plants.

Temperature Regulation:
Water helps regulate the temperature of the plant. On hot days, water can evaporate from the leaves,

cooling the plant down.

Growth:
Water is essential for the growth of new cells in the plant. Without enough water, plants can become weak and may not grow properly.

How to Water Your Herbs
Here's a step-by-step guide on how to water your herb garden:

Gather Your Tools:
Watering Can: A small watering can with a spout is perfect for gently watering your herbs. If you don't have a watering can, you can use a small cup or container.
Spray Bottle (optional): A spray bottle can be used for misting delicate plants.

Watering Techniques:
Gently Water: Pour the water slowly and gently onto the soil at the base of each plant. This helps prevent the soil from washing away and avoids damaging the plant.
Soak the Soil: Make sure the water soaks deep into the soil so that the roots can absorb it. The soil should be moist but not waterlogged.

When to Water:
Morning or Evening: It's best to water your plants in the morning or evening when it's cooler. This

reduces the amount of water lost to evaporation and helps the plants stay hydrated longer.

Check the Soil: Before watering, check the soil by sticking your finger about an inch into it. If it feels dry, it's time to water. If it feels moist, you can wait another day.

Watering Frequency:

Regular Watering: Most herbs need to be watered regularly, especially during dry or hot weather. However, different herbs have different water needs. For example, rosemary prefers drier soil, while mint likes more moisture.

Adjust for Weather: On very hot days, you might need to water your plants more often. On cooler or rainy days, you can water less frequently.

Fun Watering Activities

Here are some fun activities to do with your parents while watering your herb garden:

Watering Schedule Chart:

Create a chart to track when you water your herbs. You can draw pictures of each herb and mark the days you water them. This helps you remember which plants need watering and when.

Watering Song or Dance:

Make up a watering song or dance to do while you water your plants. This makes the activity fun and helps you remember to water gently and thoroughly.

Observation Journal:
Keep a journal to record how your plants respond to watering. Note how the leaves look before and after watering, and track the growth of your herbs. This helps you learn more about the needs of each plant.

Watering Experiment:
Conduct a simple experiment to see how different amounts of water affect plant growth. Plant two of the same herbs in separate pots, and water one more than the other. Observe the differences in their growth and health.

Signs Your Herbs Need Water
Learning to recognize when your herbs need water is important for keeping them healthy. Here are some signs to look for:

Wilting Leaves:
If the leaves start to droop or wilt, it's a sign that the plant needs water.

Dry Soil:
If the soil feels dry to the touch, it's time to water.

Yellowing Leaves:
Leaves that start to turn yellow can be a sign of underwatering (or sometimes overwatering).

Slow Growth:
If your plants are not growing as they should, they might need more water.

By watering your herbs properly and regularly, you'll help them grow strong and healthy. Your herbs will thrive, providing you with fresh flavors for your meals and a beautiful garden to enjoy.

6. Feed Your Plants

Just like you need to eat your veggies to grow big and strong, your herbs need food too! Every few weeks, your parents can help you give your herbs some special plant food to help them grow. They'll teach you how to measure the food and mix it with water to make a yummy snack for your plants. Feeding your plants is like giving them a superpower potion to help them grow tall and strong!

Why Plants Need Food
Plants need nutrients to grow just like you need food to grow strong and healthy. Here's why feeding your plants is important:

Essential Nutrients:
Plants need nutrients like nitrogen, phosphorus, and potassium (often called NPK) to stay healthy and grow.
Nitrogen helps with leaf and stem growth, phosphorus supports root development, and potassium helps with overall plant health.

Soil Nutrition:
Over time, the nutrients in the soil can get used up by the plants. Adding plant food replenishes these nutrients, ensuring your herbs have everything they need to thrive.

Healthy Growth:
Proper nutrition helps your plants grow strong, produce more leaves or flowers, and resist diseases better.

How to Feed Your Plants
Here's a step-by-step guide on how to feed your herb plants:

Choose the Right Plant Food:
There are different types of plant food or fertilizer available, such as liquid or granular forms.
Your parents can help you choose a balanced fertilizer specifically made for herbs or vegetables. Look for numbers on the package like 10-10-10, which indicate the ratio of nitrogen, phosphorus, and potassium.

Mixing Plant Food:
Follow the instructions on the plant food package. Usually, you'll mix a small amount of plant food with water in a watering can.
Stir or shake well to make sure the plant food is dissolved in the water.

Feeding Your Plants:
Pour the diluted plant food mixture directly onto the soil around your herb plants. Avoid getting the food on the leaves, as it can sometimes cause burns.
Water the plants lightly after feeding to help the nutrients soak into the soil.

Frequency:
Feed your herbs every few weeks during the growing season, typically from spring to early fall. In winter, plants grow more slowly, so they need less food.

Fun Activities While Feeding Your Plants
Here are some fun activities to do with your parents while feeding your herb garden:

Measuring Practice:
Practice measuring the plant food with a measuring cup or spoon. This helps you learn about fractions and measurements.

Science Experiment:
Set up a simple science experiment to see how different amounts of plant food affect plant growth. Use two plants of the same type, feed one with more plant food than the other, and observe the differences.

Garden Journal:
Keep a garden journal to record when you feed your

plants and how they respond. Note any changes in growth or appearance.

Signs Your Plants Need Food

Slow Growth:
If your plants are growing slowly or have stopped growing altogether, they may need more nutrients.

Yellowing Leaves:
Leaves that turn yellow, especially older leaves, can be a sign of nutrient deficiency.

Small Leaves:
If new leaves are smaller than usual, it could mean your plants need more food to grow properly.
Feeding your herbs with plant food is like giving them a special treat to help them grow strong and healthy. With the right care and nutrition, your herb garden will flourish, providing you with fresh, tasty herbs for cooking and enjoyment!

7. Watch and Wait
Now it's time to be patient and watch your herb garden grow! Your parents will help you check on your plants every day and see how they're doing. Together, you can marvel at how they get a little taller and bigger each day, just like magic! Your parents will explain how plants grow and why they need water, sunlight, and love to thrive. It's like watching a secret garden come to life right before

your eyes!

Understanding Plant Growth
Watching your plants grow is exciting and educational. Here's what happens during the growth process:

Germination:
This is when the seed starts to sprout and grow roots. It's like the plant waking up from a long sleep. You might notice tiny green shoots pushing through the soil as your herb seeds germinate.

Seedling Stage:
After germination, the seedling stage begins. The plant starts to grow leaves and develop its true shape.
Seedlings are delicate and need extra care, including gentle watering and protection from strong sunlight or pests.

Maturation:
As the plant continues to grow, it becomes stronger and develops more leaves, stems, and sometimes flowers.
Your herb plants will gradually become larger and more robust as they mature.

Daily Plant Checks
Here's how you can observe and care for your herb garden daily:

Check for Growth:
Look closely at your plants every day. Notice any changes in size, color, or new leaves sprouting.
Measure the height of your plants with a ruler or a measuring tape to see how much they've grown.

Inspect Leaves and Stems:
Check the leaves and stems for any signs of pests, like holes or discoloration. If you spot pests, let your parents know so they can help you take care of the problem.

Watering Routine:
Check the soil daily to see if it's dry. If it is, water your plants gently as you've learned before.
Observe how the soil feels after watering—moist soil is good for plants, but soggy soil might mean you're watering too much.

Fun Activities While Watching Your Plants Grow
Here are some fun activities to enjoy with your parents while watching your herb garden grow:

Plant Growth Chart:
Create a growth chart to track the progress of each herb plant. Use stickers or drawings to mark milestones like the first sprout or the first flower.

Nature Journal:
Start a nature journal where you can draw pictures

of your plants, write down observations, and note any changes you see each day.

Science Experiments:
Set up simple experiments to learn more about plants. For example, you can test how different amounts of sunlight affect plant growth by placing plants in different locations.

Plant Photography:
Take photos of your herb garden at different stages of growth. Create a photo album or scrapbook to document the journey of your plants.

Watching your herb garden grow is a wonderful experience that teaches you about nature, patience, and the magic of life. With your parents' guidance, you'll learn how to care for your plants and enjoy the rewards of fresh herbs for cooking and sharing with others.

8. Harvest Your Herbs

When your herbs are nice and big, it's time to start using them in your cooking! Your parents will show you how to snip off a few leaves or sprigs whenever you need them. Together, you can make delicious meals using your garden-fresh herbs. Your parents might even let you be the chef and cook up some tasty dishes using your homegrown herbs. It's like being a master chef with your own secret ingredients!

The Joy of Harvesting Herbs
Harvesting herbs from your garden is one of the most rewarding parts of gardening. Here's how you can enjoy harvesting your herbs:

Timing:
Herbs are best harvested in the morning, after the dew has dried but before the sun gets too hot. This is when their flavors are most concentrated.

Tools You Need:
Scissors or Pruning Shears: Use clean scissors or pruning shears to snip off herb leaves or sprigs. This helps keep your plants healthy.
Baskets or Trays: Use baskets or trays to collect the harvested herbs. This makes it easy to carry them to the kitchen.

Harvesting Technique:
Snip or Pinch: Depending on the herb, you can either snip off the leaves with scissors or pinch them off with your fingers. For woody herbs like rosemary, use scissors to avoid damaging the plant.

Leave Some Behind:
When harvesting, leave some leaves on the plant so it can continue to grow and produce more herbs. This ensures a continuous supply throughout the growing season.

Cooking with Your Herbs
Here are some fun ways to use your garden-fresh herbs in cooking:

Fresh Salads: Add chopped basil, parsley, or cilantro to salads for a burst of flavor and freshness.

Flavorful Pasta: Stir freshly chopped herbs like thyme or oregano into pasta sauces for extra flavor.

Herb Butter: Mix finely chopped herbs with softened butter to create herb butter. Spread it on bread or use it to cook vegetables or meats.

Infused Water or Tea: Make refreshing drinks by adding mint or lemon balm leaves to water or steeping them for herbal tea.

Learning About Flavors
Explore the flavors of different herbs with your parents:

Taste Testing: Try tasting each herb by itself to experience its unique flavor. Talk about how each herb tastes—some might be spicy, others minty, or even slightly sweet.

Smelling Herbs: Smell the herbs before using them. Some herbs have strong aromas that can tell you what flavors they'll add to your food.

Experimenting: Get creative with your cooking. Try mixing different herbs together to create new flavors in your dishes.

Sharing Your Harvest
Share the joy of your homegrown herbs with others:

Cooking Together: Invite friends or family to cook with you using your garden-fresh herbs. Share your favorite recipes and enjoy the delicious meals together.

Gifts: Package fresh herbs in small baskets or jars to give as gifts to friends, family, or neighbors. It's a thoughtful way to share your garden's bounty.

Herb Tasting Party: Host a tasting party where everyone can try dishes made with your homegrown herbs. It's a fun way to showcase your gardening skills!

Preserving Herbs
If you have more herbs than you can use right away, here's how you can preserve them for later:

Drying Herbs: Tie herb bundles together and hang them upside down in a cool, dry place. Once dry, store the leaves in airtight containers.

Freezing Herbs: Chop herbs and place them in ice

cube trays filled with water or olive oil. Once frozen, transfer the cubes to freezer bags for easy use later.

Harvesting and cooking with your homegrown herbs is a wonderful way to connect with nature, explore flavors, and enjoy delicious meals with your family. With each harvest, you'll discover new ways to use herbs and appreciate the magic of growing your own food.

Learning and Fun
Growing an herb garden is not only fun but also a great way to learn about nature and science. You'll discover how plants grow, what they need to stay healthy, and how they can be used in cooking and medicine. You'll also learn important skills like patience, responsibility, and how to take care of living things. Plus, you'll have the satisfaction of growing your own food and sharing it with others.

So, my dear young herbalists, are you ready to start your herbal adventure? With a little help from your parents, you'll soon have a thriving herb garden filled with delicious and magical herbs.

RESPECTING NATURE

When we grow herbs, we're like nature's helpers, taking care of the plants and helping them grow big and strong. But with great power, like having a special garden, comes great responsibility! Imagine if every superhero had a rule they had to follow to make sure they used their powers for good. Well, our rule as herb gardeners is to respect nature and take care of the Earth. Just like how we treat our friends with kindness, we want to treat nature with kindness too!

Sustainable Harvesting

Harvesting with Care:
Harvesting herbs sustainably means being careful not to take too much from the plants all at once. Just like you wouldn't take all the toys from a friend,

we leave enough leaves on the plant so it can keep growing.

Only take what you need for cooking or making remedies, and leave some leaves behind to help the plant stay healthy and keep producing more herbs.

Giving Back to the Earth:

After harvesting, we can give back to the Earth by composting leftover plant parts. Composting is like giving the Earth a yummy snack—it helps create nutrient-rich soil for more plants to grow.

Recycling pots and tools when they're old or no longer needed helps reduce waste and keeps our gardens eco-friendly.

Being Good Stewards

Kindness to Nature:

Just like how we say thank you to someone who helps us, we can say thank you to the Earth by taking care of our herb garden and keeping it healthy.

Watering our plants gently, keeping them free from pests, and making sure they have enough sunlight are all ways to show kindness to our plants and nature.

Thinking About the Future:

By being good stewards of the Earth and showing kindness to nature, we're making sure that future generations—like our brothers, sisters, and friends —can continue to benefit from the magic of herbalism.

It's like passing on a special gift to the people we love, so they can enjoy growing and using herbs just like we do.

Our Superhero Rule
Responsibility:

1. Remember, with great power comes great responsibility. As herb gardeners, our superpower is caring for plants and nature.

2. Let's be kind to nature, harvest our herbs sustainably by only taking what we need, and give back to the Earth through composting and recycling.

Enjoying Herbalism for Years to Come:

By following these rules and showing kindness to nature, we ensure that we can keep enjoying the wonders of herbalism for many, many years. It's like protecting a treasure that brings us joy and health. Respecting nature and being kind to the Earth is not just good for our herb gardens—it's good for the whole world around us. Let's continue to be nature's helpers and enjoy the magic of growing herbs responsibly!

HERBALISM AROUND THE WORLD

I magine embarking on a fascinating journey across continents to explore how different cultures harness the power of herbs for healing and wellness. Each stop on our adventure unveils unique traditions and centuries-old wisdom passed down through generations.

China

In China, herbalism is deeply rooted in a holistic system of healthcare known as Traditional Chinese Medicine (TCM), which has been practiced for thousands of years. TCM emphasizes the balance of energies within the body to achieve health and wellness.

The Concept of Qi

Central to TCM is the concept of Qi (pronounced "chee"), which is the vital energy that flows through our bodies. Chinese herbalists believe that illness occurs when Qi is out of balance or blocked. Herbs are used to restore this balance and promote healing.

Diversity of Herbs

Chinese herbalists have a treasure trove of herbs at their disposal, each chosen for its specific healing properties. For example:

Ginseng: Known for boosting energy and improving stamina.

Ginger: Used to aid digestion and reduce nausea.

Goji berries: Rich in antioxidants and used to improve immune function.

These herbs are not only used individually but also combined in teas, soups, and complex herbal formulas tailored to address each person's unique health needs.

Preservation of Knowledge

The wisdom of Chinese herbalism is preserved through ancient texts like the "Shennong Ben Cao Jing," which catalogues hundreds of herbs and their medicinal uses. This knowledge is passed down through generations of practitioners who study under experienced herbalists, learning the art of herb selection, preparation, and application.

Application in Daily Life

In Chinese culture, herbal remedies are integrated into daily life as a natural way to maintain health and prevent illness. Families may brew herbal teas or soups based on TCM principles to support overall well-being.

By understanding Chinese herbalism and TCM, we gain insight into a holistic approach to health that considers the interconnectedness of the body's energies and the healing power of nature's herbs. This ancient practice continues to thrive, offering valuable lessons in wellness and natural medicine for generations to come.

North America

Native American cultures across North America have a deep spiritual connection with nature, viewing plants as sacred gifts that hold medicinal and ceremonial significance. Let's explore how herbs are used and revered within these rich traditions.

Spiritual Significance of Plants

Plants like sage, cedar, and sweetgrass hold special importance in Native American cultures. They are believed to embody the essence of the Creator and are used in ceremonies to cleanse and purify spaces, individuals, and objects. For example:

Sage: Used in smudging ceremonies to clear negative energy and promote healing.

Cedar: Burned as incense to purify and protect, often used in blessing rituals.

Sweetgrass: Braided and burned to invite positive energies and bless ceremonies.

Medicinal Uses

Beyond their spiritual roles, these plants are also valued for their medicinal properties:

Sage tea: Used to treat sore throats and respiratory infections.

Cedar poultices: Applied to wounds to prevent infection and promote healing.

Sweetgrass tea: Consumed for its calming effects and to aid digestion.

Each tribe has its own herbal knowledge passed down through generations, with elders and healers playing a crucial role in preserving and transmitting this wisdom orally. Traditional healers understand the specific uses of local plants and their holistic approach to healing, addressing physical, mental, and spiritual well-being.

Preservation of Traditional Knowledge

The transmission of herbal knowledge is part of an oral tradition, where stories, rituals, and practices are shared through storytelling and apprenticeships. This ensures that each community's unique understanding of herbal medicine continues to thrive, adapting to modern challenges while maintaining cultural integrity.

Cultural Integration

Herbalism is deeply integrated into daily life and ceremonial practices among Native American tribes, reflecting a profound respect for nature and its healing powers. By honoring plants as sacred gifts, these cultures uphold a harmonious relationship with the natural world and teach valuable lessons in sustainability and holistic wellness.

Native American herbalism offers a holistic perspective on health, emphasizing the interconnectedness of mind, body, spirit, and the natural environment. Through their traditional practices, Native tribes demonstrate profound wisdom in using plants not only for physical healing but also for spiritual and cultural enrichment. This ancient knowledge continues to inspire respect for nature and the preservation of indigenous cultures for future generations.

India

In India, Ayurveda is more than just a system of medicine—it's a way of life that seeks to harmonize the mind, body, and spirit through holistic practices and herbal remedies. Let's delve into the fascinating world of Ayurveda and its principles of health and wellness.

Principles of Ayurveda

Ayurveda teaches that each person is unique, with a specific constitution known as a dosha. There are three main doshas:

Vata: Associated with air and ether elements, governing movement and communication.

Pitta: Linked to fire and water elements, responsible for digestion and metabolism.

Kapha: Influenced by earth and water elements, regulating stability and structure.

According to Ayurvedic principles, health is maintained when these doshas are in balance, and illness arises when there is an imbalance. Herbs play a vital role in restoring this balance.

Key Ayurvedic Herbs

Ayurvedic practitioners utilize a wide array of herbs, each selected for its specific properties:

Turmeric: Known for its anti-inflammatory and antioxidant properties, used to support joint health and overall vitality.

Neem: Used for its antibacterial and cleansing properties, beneficial for skin health and immune support.

Ashwagandha: Adaptogenic herb that helps manage stress, enhance stamina, and promote mental clarity.

These herbs are often prepared in various forms, including herbal teas, powders, and complex formulations called rasayanas, which are tailored to address specific health concerns and doshic imbalances.

Treatment Approaches

Ayurvedic treatment is personalized, taking into account not only physical symptoms but also mental and emotional states. Practitioners diagnose imbalances through detailed assessments, pulse readings, and observation of bodily characteristics.

Holistic Lifestyle Practices

Ayurveda encompasses more than herbal remedies. It promotes a holistic lifestyle that includes:

Diet: Emphasizing fresh, seasonal foods that support each dosha.

Yoga and Meditation: Practices to cultivate physical strength, mental clarity, and spiritual well-being.

Daily Routine (Dinacharya): Establishing habits that align with natural rhythms to promote balance and vitality.

Preservation of Ancient Wisdom

Ancient Ayurvedic texts like the "Charaka Samhita" and "Sushruta Samhita" serve as foundational guides, preserving centuries-old knowledge of herbs, treatments, and lifestyle practices. This wisdom is passed down through generations of practitioners, ensuring the continuity and efficacy of Ayurvedic medicine.

Ayurveda offers a profound understanding of health and wellness, integrating herbal medicine with lifestyle practices to achieve harmony within oneself and with the natural world. By embracing Ayurvedic principles, individuals can enhance their overall well-being and cultivate a deeper connection to their innate healing capacities.

Africa

In Africa, herbalism is deeply intertwined with the continent's diverse ecosystems and cultural traditions, offering a holistic approach to healing that honors the interconnectedness of people and nature. Let's explore the fascinating world of African herbalism and its profound significance.

Plants of Significance

African herbalism encompasses a vast array of plants, each cherished for its unique healing properties and cultural importance:

Rooibos: Known for its antioxidant-rich leaves used to make a soothing tea that supports overall health.

Buchu: Utilized for its anti-inflammatory and diuretic properties, beneficial for treating urinary tract infections and digestive issues.

Hoodia: Traditionally used to suppress appetite and provide sustenance during long journeys in the desert regions of Southern Africa.

These plants not only address physical ailments but also play pivotal roles in spiritual ceremonies, promoting harmony and balance within communities.

Role of Traditional Healers

Traditional healers, known as sangomas or

herbalists, hold esteemed positions in African societies, serving as healers, spiritual guides, and custodians of cultural wisdom. They possess extensive knowledge of local flora and the therapeutic uses of plants, acquired through oral traditions passed down through generations.

Healing Rituals and Practices

Herbal remedies in Africa are often prepared through sacred rituals that honor the interconnectedness of people and nature. For example:

Harvesting: Plants are gathered with respect, acknowledging their role as gifts from the earth.

Preparation: Herbs may be dried, brewed into teas, or applied topically as poultices to treat various ailments.

Spiritual Ceremonies: Healing rituals may involve chanting, drumming, and offerings to invoke the spiritual energies of plants.

These practices not only address physical illnesses but also spiritual and emotional imbalances, recognizing the holistic nature of human health.

Cultural Transmission

The knowledge of African herbalism is transmitted through oral traditions, where elders and experienced healers pass down their wisdom to younger generations through storytelling and apprenticeships. This ensures the preservation of traditional healing practices and the continuity of cultural heritage.

Environmental Stewardship

African herbalism promotes environmental stewardship by fostering a deep respect for the natural world. Traditional healers emphasize sustainable harvesting practices, ensuring that plants are gathered responsibly to preserve biodiversity and maintain ecological balance.

African herbalism embodies a profound understanding of health and well-being, integrating medicinal plants with spiritual practices to promote holistic healing. By embracing these ancient traditions, African communities nurture a harmonious relationship with nature and uphold cultural resilience for future generations to cherish and benefit from.

Europe

Europe has a vibrant history of herbalism that spans centuries, rooted in the use of plants for medicinal, culinary, and spiritual purposes. Let's embark on a journey through the rich tapestry of European herbal traditions and their enduring significance.

Ancient Roots of Herbalism

Herbalism in Europe dates back to ancient times, where plants such as chamomile, lavender, and peppermint played vital roles in daily life:

Chamomile: Known for its calming properties, used in teas to promote relaxation and soothe digestive discomfort.

Lavender: Revered for its aromatic scent and medicinal benefits, applied in oils and sachets to ease headaches and aid sleep.

Peppermint: Valued for its refreshing taste and digestive support, enjoyed in teas and culinary dishes.

These herbs were cultivated in monastery gardens, tended by monks who meticulously studied their medicinal properties and recorded their uses in manuscripts.

Traditions and Practices

European herbalism encompasses diverse regional traditions shaped by local landscapes and cultural practices:

Wise Women and Herbalists: Throughout history, wise women and herbalists were esteemed for their knowledge of plants, passing down herbal remedies through oral traditions and practical teachings.

Monastic Gardens: Monks cultivated medicinal herbs in monastery gardens, blending spiritual practices with herbal knowledge to care for both body and soul.

Folk Remedies: Each region developed unique folk remedies, using local plants and traditions to treat common ailments and promote well-being.

Renaissance of European Herbalism

In recent years, there has been a resurgence of interest in European herbalism as people rediscover the benefits of natural remedies:

Natural Alternatives: Many individuals seek herbal alternatives to modern medicines, appreciating the gentle yet effective nature of herbal treatments.

Herbal Gardens: Community and home gardens now thrive with medicinal herbs, connecting people to their cultural heritage and the healing power of plants.

Integration into Modern Life: Herbal practices are integrated into contemporary lifestyles through teas, herbal supplements, and natural skincare products, offering holistic approaches to health and wellness.

Preservation of Heritage

The revival of European herbalism honors ancestral wisdom while adapting to modern needs:

Educational Initiatives: Schools and herbal workshops teach about local plants and their traditional uses, ensuring that herbal knowledge is passed on to future generations.

Environmental Awareness: Herbalists emphasize sustainable harvesting practices and conservation efforts to protect native plant species and biodiversity.

European herbalism embodies a deep reverence for nature and the healing potential of plants, blending ancient wisdom with modern sensibilities. By embracing herbal traditions, individuals cultivate a deeper connection to their heritage and the natural world, fostering holistic well-being for themselves and future generations. As we continue to explore and appreciate European herbalism, we celebrate its enduring legacy and its ongoing contribution to health, harmony, and cultural richness.

Connecting Cultures through Herbalism

Exploring herbalism across these diverse cultures reveals a universal reverence for nature and a shared understanding of plants' profound healing potential. Each tradition emphasizes sustainability, respect for biodiversity, and the holistic integration of mind, body, and spirit in health care practices. By learning from these global perspectives, we deepen our appreciation for the interconnectedness of cultures and the importance of preserving traditional knowledge for future generations. Herbalism transcends geographical boundaries, offering valuable insights into sustainable living, wellness practices, and the profound relationship between humans and the natural world.

HERBALISM IN EVERYDAY LIFE

Now that we've learned about herbalism from around the world, let's see how we can make it a part of our own lives, every day!

1. Herbal Tea

Herbal teas are a fun and tasty way to enjoy the benefits of plants:

Choosing Herbs: Each herb has its own special flavor and health benefits. For example:

Chamomile is great for relaxing and helps you fall asleep. It's like a warm hug for your tummy!

Peppermint is refreshing and can help if your stomach feels upset.

Lemon Balm has a zesty taste that can make you feel

happier and more energized.

Making Tea: Here's how to make your own herbal tea:

Boil Water: Ask your parents to help you boil water in a pot or kettle.

Add Herbs: Put your chosen herbs into a teapot or cup. You can use fresh leaves or dried herbs.

Steep the Tea: Pour the hot water over the herbs and let them sit for about 5-10 minutes. The longer you let them steep, the stronger the flavor will be!

Strain and Serve: Use a strainer to remove the herbs, then pour your tea into a mug. You can add a little honey or lemon for extra flavor.

Why It's Good for You: Drinking herbal tea can be relaxing and help with many things, like calming your nerves or soothing your tummy. Plus, it's a great way to stay hydrated with a tasty twist!

2. Essential Oils

Essential oils are like tiny bottles of plant magic that can make your home smell wonderful and help you feel good:

What Are Essential Oils? Essential oils are made from the essence of plants, capturing their fragrance and beneficial properties. Some popular ones include:

Lavender is calming and great for helping you relax before bedtime.

Peppermint can give you a boost of energy and help you stay focused.

Eucalyptus is refreshing and helps you breathe easier.

Using Essential Oils:

In a Diffuser: Ask your parents to help you add a few drops of lavender oil to a diffuser with water. Turn it on, and soon your room will smell like a beautiful garden!

On Your Skin: Mix a few drops of essential oil with a carrier oil, like coconut oil, and rub it on your wrists or temples. This way, you can carry the soothing scent with you all day.

Fun Fact: Essential oils can help you feel calm, energized, or even help you sleep better. It's like having a little piece of nature with you wherever you go!

3. Cooking with Fresh Herbs

Cooking with fresh herbs is a tasty way to add flavor and health benefits to your meals:

Herb Selection: Herbs like basil, rosemary, thyme, and cilantro can make your food taste amazing. Here's how to use them:

Basil goes great with tomatoes and makes your pizza taste extra yummy.

Rosemary adds a delicious flavor to roasted potatoes.

Mint can be added to desserts or drinks for a refreshing taste.

How to Use Herbs in Cooking:

Wash and Chop: Ask your parents to help you wash and chop the herbs. Make sure you know the difference between the leaves and stems.

Add to Dishes: Sprinkle chopped herbs on your meals. You can mix them into salads, soups, or even desserts for a burst of flavor.

Health Benefits: Herbs are packed with vitamins, minerals, and antioxidants that can help keep you healthy. They add flavor without extra salt or sugar, making your meals tastier and healthier!

4. Exploring Nature

Going on a nature walk can be an exciting adventure, where you might find herbs growing all around you:

Finding Herbs: Look for plants like dandelions, clover, and plantain in your yard or at a park. These plants are not just weeds—they have special uses!

Dandelions can be made into tea or used in salads.

Clover flowers are sweet and can be added to drinks for a little flavor.

Plantain leaves can be used to soothe bee stings or minor cuts.

How to Use Herbs in Nature:

Identify Plants: With the help of your parents, learn how to identify different herbs. Use a plant guidebook or an app to help you.

Practical Uses: You can make dandelion tea, use plantain leaves to help with insect bites, or just enjoy the smell of fresh herbs.

Benefits of Nature: Spending time outside is good for your body and mind. It helps you feel calm and connected to the earth. Plus, it's a great way to learn about the plants and animals that share our world!

Educational Insights of Herbalism

Botanical Basics: Introduce simple science concepts like how plants grow, the parts of a plant (roots, stems, leaves, flowers), and what they need to survive (water, sunlight, soil).

Cultural Connection: Learn about how different cultures use herbs, and discuss how these traditions have influenced our modern practices.

Environmental Care: Talk about the importance of taking care of our planet. Discuss sustainable practices like planting herbs, composting, and reducing waste. Explain how these actions help protect our environment for future generations.

Incorporating herbal remedies into your daily routine is a fun and educational way to explore nature and enhance your well-being. Whether you're sipping herbal tea, diffusing essential oils, cooking with fresh herbs, or discovering plants on a nature walk, herbalism offers a world of possibilities. It's like having a magical toolkit of plants that can make you feel happy, healthy, and connected to the world around you. So, get curious, have fun, and let the wonders of herbs bring a little bit of magic into your everyday life!

THE MAGIC OF HERBALISM

As we reach the end of our incredible journey through the world of herbs and plants, let's pause to celebrate the amazing wonders nature has to offer! From the tiny herbs peeking out in our gardens to the special potions made by healers all over, plants are like nature's own superheroes, ready to help us stay happy and strong.

Throughout our adventure, we've seen so many fascinating things! We learned about herbs from faraway places like China, where they have special powers to help us feel better when we're not well. Then we visited Native American lands, where plants are like celebrities in their healing ceremonies, used to make people feel better in their hearts and minds. In India, they use herbs to keep everything in balance, like a tightrope walker on a circus rope. And in Africa and Europe, people have been using herbs for centuries to make yummy food taste even better and help us feel our best.

Now that we've discovered all these amazing ways people use herbs, it's time for us to become little herbalists ourselves! Imagine being able to make your own delicious tea, using herbs like a secret recipe. Or smelling oils that make you feel like you're walking through a flower garden, even if you're just in your own room. You could even cook with fresh herbs and feel like a real chef, adding magic to your meals!

So, let's embrace our inner herbalists, my friends! Let's keep our eyes wide open to the enchanting wonders of nature's medicine cabinet. And remember, sharing is caring—so don't forget to tell your friends and family about all the cool things you've learned. Together, we can spread the magic of plants and make the world a happier, healthier place!

ABOUT THE AUTHOR

Emily Kate Adams

 Emily Kate Adams is a certified master herbalist with a passion for plants and education. She created "Herbal Explorers" to inspire children to grow herbs and learn about herbalism. Through her book, she shares her expertise and love for the natural world, encouraging curiosity and connection with the wonders of herbs.

Printed in Great Britain
by Amazon

53368700R00056